Growing the Hallucinogens

How to Cultivate and Harvest Legal Psychoactive Plants

by Hudson Grubber

T0165958

20TH CENTURY ALCHEMIST

Growing the Hallucinogens
ISBN 0-914171-47-X
ISBN 978-0-914171-47-8
Copyright 1973 and 1991 by 20th Century Alchemist

Published by
Ronin Publishing, Inc.
PO Box 22900
Oakland CA 94609

Originally published by High Times/Level Press in 1971

Published in the United States of America

Cover Design: Bonnie Smetts
Cover Photograph: Harlan Ang

DISCLAIMER:
This book is offered for sale solely for educational and informaitional purposes. The author and publisher advocate no illegal activities of any kind, and make no express or implied warranties of merchantability, fitness for any purpose, or otherwise, with respect to this book. For medical, legal, or spiritual advise, we urge that the reader consult appropriate practitioners.

Growing
the
Hallucinogens

CONTENTS

INTRODUCTION

The purpose of this book is to introduce the reader to the general arts of plant cultivation and propagation, and to give specific information on growing certain psychoactive plants.

For each plant we give a brief description, and the methods of cultivation, propagation, and harvesting.

There are sections on general propagation and cultivation techniques in the beginning of the book. Propagation has been stressed because adequate information is often lacking in garden books. These sections explain the terminology used in the information found under each plant.

A list of suppliers of seeds, cuttings, and dried herbs may be found on page 71.

Complete information on the preparation, dosage, use, active constituents, effects and side effects of the plant materials discussed in this book can be found in another publication from the Twentieth Century Alchemist entitled *Legal Highs*.

At the time of this writing, the plants covered in this book are legal. It may interest some readers that the Church of the Tree of Life has declared as religious sacraments most of the plants in this book, thereby protecting its members from any future legislation involving these plants. Those seeking further information should send a stamped, self-addressed envelope to the Church of the Tree of Life, 405 Columbus Avenue, San Francisco, California 94133.

Some of the plants discussed in *Legal Highs* and *Growing the Hallucinogens* contain substances which are forbidden by law. As examples, San Pedro contains mescaline, and morning glory and Hawaiian wood rose seeds contain lysergic acid amides. The general application of the law appears to be that it is legal for a person to cultivate these plants, as long as no steps are taken that could be interpreted as intent to ingest them for psychoactive effects.

This book is about gardening. It contains accurate information on the cultivation and harvesting of the plants in question. It should not be construed as encouragement or endorsement of the use of these plants for hallucinogenic purposes.

I wish to thank my wife for typing this manuscript.

H.G.

PROPAGATION

Propagation is the reproduction of plants, and is accomplished by two different means. One is by seeds or spores (the normal reproductive process of plants), the other is by vegetative propagation, which involves cuttings, layers, division, separation, or graftings.

SEEDS

The seeds of many annuals will germinate (sprout) readily when sown directly in the ground in spring. Other plants have seeds with hard seedcoats or dormancies that must be broken before they will grow. Methods of doing so include:

Nicking and Soaking: Large seeds often benefit from soaking in water overnight or *until swollen*. Some seeds, such as the mescal bean and large woodrose, will refuse to swell unless the seed coat is nicked or scratched first. With a knife, small file, or hacksaw blade, scrape away a small portion of the seedcoat on the side opposite the hilum or germ eye (the small dent where the seed sprouts). The hole should not be big, just large enough for water to enter during soaking.

3

When soaking any seed, be sure to plant it as soon as it is swollen, as some seeds will drown if left for long in the water.

Stratification: Some seeds need to be stratified before they will germinate. This process involves placing the seed in damp peat moss or sand, and storing at a low temperature until dormancy is broken.

Chemicals: Chemicals are sometimes used for seeds with hard seedcoats that are not affected by stratification or soaking. In nature, these seeds have their coats softened by the digestive juices of birds and animals that eat them. Acids such as vinegar or sulfuric acid, and alkalies like sodium hypochlorite (Clorox) are used. The seeds must be thoroughly washed after treatment.

Scalding Seeds: Other hard-shelled seeds, particularly in the bean family, are best treated with boiling water. To do this, place the seeds in a teacup, and pour boiling water over them. The water is allowed to cool and the seeds are soaked until they swell. This may be repeated with any seed that does not swell after the first time.

Peat Moss: This is a very good medium in which to sprout seeds. Put some milled sphagnum moss (peat moss) in a plastic bag. Add water and knead thoroughly until the moss is uniformly damp. Fill a shallow pan or aluminum pie tin about 1 inch deep with the damp moss. Cover with plastic wrap, or a sheet of glass. Seeds may be started on the surface of the moss or buried in it; with or without bottom heat.

Bottom Heat: This hastens germination of many seeds. To provide bottom heat, take a strong corrugated cardboard box and turn it upside down with a 40-watt light inside. Cut slits or small holes in the bottom to let the heat through to the flats or seed pans. Be sure that the heat will not cook the seedlings, as different seed pans or flats transmit different amounts of heat.

When sowing seeds a general rule is to cover them with soil 2 or 3 times their thickness. Very small seeds, like coleus or tobacco, should be just slightly covered or pressed into the surface. Small seeds may also be mixed with sand to insure even distribution.

The soil for all seeds should be light and porous.

Seedlings should be transplanted after the second pair of true leaves opens. Transplanting is preferably done on a cool cloudy day. The transplant should be shaded for several days.

VEGETATIVE PROPAGATION

Hardwood Cuttings: These are cuttings of dormant twigs or stems of woody plants. Such a cutting is usually taken in fall or winter. There should be 2 to 4 nodes or buds on the stem. This is inserted at an angle in sand, peat moss, or a combination of the two, with only the top bud projecting. It is then left in a cool place where it will not freeze, for the duration of winter. During this time the lower end will heal over or callus. In the spring, it is planted in a sandy soil where it will root readily, especially if the lower buds are removed.

Greenwood Cuttings: These are cuttings made of shoots of plants that are mature enough to break when bent sharply. These cuttings are rooted indoors in sand, gravel, or sandy peat moss almost up to the lower leaves. The lower leaves are often removed or cut to reduce the area exposed to air and so prevent wilting. The cuttings should have some leaves, though, as this will help them to root faster. They should be shaded and have gentle bottom heat. Many herbaceous plants maybe rooted in water. When rooting this way, never place the cuttings in more than 2 inches of water, as deep water does not absorb enough exygen for good root development. If the cutting wilts, clip the leaves in half to reduce surface area, or placed a jar upside down over it. Rootone, a rooting hormone, may be used to hasten root growth. Plants from which cuttings are to be taken should receive plenty of sunlight for several days before the cutting is made. This builds up the sugar-energy storage and improves the success of the cutting.

Root Cuttings: These may be taken from any plant that produces sprouts from the roots. They are made from roots the thickness of a pencil to ½ inch thick, and 3 to 5 inches long. They need not show buds as buds will develop later. They are treated similarly to hardwood cuttings except that in the spring they are placed horizontally in the soil and entirely covered to a depth of 1 to 2 inches.

Ground Layering: This is a method of rooting shoots while they are still attached to the parent plant. It is often used with plants whose cuttings refuse to root. Select a low-growing branch that can be bent to the ground. Make a slanting cut half-way through the branch at a point about 12 inches from the end, and just below a joint. Then wedge it open with a pebble. Bury the cut in about 4 inches of soil and anchor it with a stone. Stake up the end of the branch so that it extends above the soil line. Keep the soil moist, and carefully dig down to the cut every few months to check if rooting has taken place. Once rooted, the branch may be severed from the parent plant and grown like an ordinary cutting.

Air Layering: This is similar to ground layering but may be done with any branch. Select a branch from pencil size up to one inch thick. Make a slanting cut half-way through the branch. Wedge the cut open with a matchstick and dust the cut lightly with rooting hormone. With thick branches, a ring of bark should be removed instead of cutting the branch. Surround it with a handful of damp peat moss and enclose it with plastic wrap. Tie the wrap at both ends with wire tape. The peat moss should be kept damp. Check it frequently during the summer. In a month or two roots will form and the branch may be severed and treated like an ordinary cutting.

Division: This is the process of dividing plants that have root stocks or tubers, or which produce suckers (young plants rising from the base of the older plants). This may be achieved by breaking up large clumps of plants such as heliotrope, or cutting tubers or root-stocks into sections containing buds, as is done with potatoes or hops. Division is usually performed during the dormant season.

Separation: This is a form of division. It is the process of separating bulblets from the main bulb in the same way garlic is propagated, and setting them out to be new plants.

CULTIVATION

When cultivating plants make sure that your soil has been well worked and has been fertilized properly. The addition of humus, sand, or compost assures a workable soil.

Start seedlings in flats and transplant when a few leaves have formed. Transplanting is best done on an overcast, cool, cloudy or foggy day. Keep the roots intact as much as possible and perform your repotting swiftly and gently. Water thoroughly and shade the plant for a few days.

Do not overwater your plants. Water them thoroughly and deeply but infrequently. The roots draw upon water 1 foot or more below the surface; therefore the wetness of the soil's surface is not important. I have found that the most common cause of death among house plants is overwatering.

Volumes have been written on the basics of plant cultivation. Your local library will have many good books on the subject.

Plants should be grown with joy in one's heart and with calmness in one's actions. If you dislike your plants or the responsibility they represent they will often refuse to grow.

If you like your plants and treat them as your friends, they will respond favorably and not mind as much when you use them for your purposes. In controlled experiments under laboratory conditions it has been demonstrated that plants react to people's emotions. Plants that were treated with affection grew faster and larger than those that were not.

PESTICIDES

The subject of pesticides is too involved to discuss here. A very good pamphlet entitled *Pesticides and Your Environment* has been put out by the National Wildlife Federation (see Suppliers). It tells sources of ladybugs, praying mantises, and lacewings (all beneficial insects), gives information on companion planting, and has lists of desirable and undesirable pesticides.

This pamphlet suggests that nicotine sulfate not be used. This is due to its highly poisonous nature, rather than because of any damage to the environment. Otherwise this insectside has the advantage that it evaporates completely, leaving no residue.

Isopropyl (rubbing) alcohol has been used as a spray, but it can "burn" tender plants. If used it should be tested on a few leaves first. If the leaves wither in a few days, another pesticide must be used.

The Hallucinogens

THE HALLUCINOGENS

BELLADONNA
Atropa belladonna L.;
Nightshade family (Solanaceae)

A perennial branching herb growing to 5 feet tall, with 8-inch-long ovate leaves. The leaves in first-year plants are larger than those of older plants. The flowers are bell-shaped, blue-purple or dull red, followed by a shiny, black or purple ½-inch berry. Native of Europe and Asia.

Cultivation and Propagation: Belladonna is hardy throughout the U.S., dying back in winter and rising from the root in spring. It prefers a well-drained, well-limed soil in full sun or part shade. The soil should be kept moist at all times. Plants exposed to too much sun will be stunted. In hot sunny areas it may be grown between rows of beans to shade it.

Belladonna is most frequently propagated by seed, sown in flats in early March. Because the seeds take 4–6 weeks to germinate, they should be started early. When the seedlings are an inch or so high they may be set out 18 inches apart. The seedlings should be well watered just after transplanting, and shaded for several days. First-year plants will grow only 1½ feet high and will flower in September. At this time the leaves and tops may be collected, but the plants should not be entirely stripped. The plants should be thinned to 2½–3 feet apart at the approach of winter, or over-crowding will occur the second year. In June of the second year the plants may be cut to one inch above the ground when they are in flower. In good years a second crop will be ready for harvesting in September. The roots may be harvested in the autumn of the fourth year, and new plants set in their places. Belladonna may also be propagated by cuttings of the green branch tips.

I have found that snails, aphids, and white flies are among this plant's worst enemies.

Small children are much more susceptible to belladonna poisoning than adults, and should be kept away from it.

Harvesting: The parts harvested as described above should be dried quickly in the sun. Wilted or discolored leaves may be discarded, as they contain only small amounts of alkaloids.

BETEL NUT
Areca catechu L.; Palm family (Palmaceae)

A very slender, graceful palm growing up to 100 feet tall but with a trunk only 6 inches in diameter. This is topped by a crown of 3–6-foot-long leaves that are divided into many leaflets. The fruits are the size and shape of a hen's egg and are yellowish to scarlet with a fibrous covering. Native to Malaysia.

Cultivation and Propagation: May be grown out of doors in California and Florida; must be grown in the greenhouse elsewhere. Young plants do well in a mixture of equal parts leaf-mold or peat and loam. Water at least every other day. If grown in the greenhouse, the temperature should be around 80°F during the day and about 60°F at night.

Harvesting: Betel nuts should be harvested when the fruits are ripe. The acorn-sized nut is removed and washed free of pulp. An adult tree may produce 250 nuts per year.

THE BROOMS
Bean family (Leguminosae)

There is some confusion as to which is the most potent of the three species of brooms used for their psychotropic effects. According to the paper first reporting the discovery of the effects of these plants, the blossoms of Canary Island broom were the "most pleasant and effective" of the three. This is also the species used by Yaqui shamans. Some herbals claim that Spanish broom tops are five times as strong as Scotch broom, while other sources claim that the alkaloid content of the Scotch broom is higher than that of the other two. To clarify (or confuse) the issue, it has been found that alkaloid content varies with environment.

Canary Island Broom (*Cytisus canariensis* L., formerly *Genista canariensis*). A much-branched shrub to 6 feet tall with hairy branches, covered with bright green leaves divided into 3 leaflets. This is the only broom of the three that keeps its leaves through the year. It flowers from May to July, and is covered with many bright yellow blossoms in short racemes. It is damaged at 15°F but it recovers quickly. Native to the Canary Islands.

Scotch Broom (*Cytisus scoparius* L.). A shrub to 10 feet with many erect, slender, almost leafless branches. The flowers are yellow, ¾-inch long, and bloom from March to June. Native to central and southern Europe; naturalized in California and found sparingly in the East.

Spanish Broom (*Spartium junceum* L.). A shrub to 10 feet high with slender green branches and bearing a few small leaves. The flowers are yellow, 1 inch long, and fragrant, followed by 4-inch-long pods. Blooms from June to September in most of the U.S. In California it flowers most of the year. Native to the Mediterranean region.

Cultivation and Propagation: The brooms need a well-drained soil and full sun. They often naturalize on dry, rocky slopes in the west. Scotch and Spanish broom are hardy everywhere except in the most northern states, while Canary Island broom is hardy only in the west and south. All are very drought-resistant.

Brooms are easily propagated by seeds, cuttings, and layers. Seeds may be started as early as January. They should be nicked and soaked until swollen before sowing. Seedlings should be transplanted carefully when young; they transplant well when older. Plants grown from seed will flower 1 year from sowing. Cuttings should be young growth taken with a heel in early spring or August and September. They should be rooted in sandy soil. When grown as a pot or tub plant, they should be pruned after flowering. They should be left outdoors from early spring until light frost in the fall. Brooms are subject to attack by the genista worm in southern California. These are difficult to control except with DDT.

Harvesting: Broom plants grown in full sun have a higher alkaloid content than those grown in the shade. The flowers should be gathered, aged in a sealed jar for 10 days, and dried at a low heat. The aging greatly reduces the harshness of the smoke. The active flowering tops may be gathered in May and dried without aging. Any material from pruning may also be used.

CABEZA DE ANGEL

Calliandra anomala (Kunth) Macbride; Bean family (Leguminosae)

Cultivation and Propagation: It may be grown out of doors in California and the South, and in the greenhouse in the North. It needs plenty of water and sunshine and will do well in a good garden soil. If grown indoors it should be pruned after blooming and set out of doors for the summer.

Propagation is by seeds, which may require nicking and soaking before germination will take place. When seeds are not available it may be propagated by cuttings taken with a heel and planted in sand over bottom heat.

Harvesting: Incisions are made in the bark in the early morning and the exuding resin is collected after several days, dried and pulverized. The incisions should be shallow and narrow so that they will heal quickly. Take care not to cut too deep as this may permanently damage the plant.

CALAMUS
Acorus calamus L.; Arum family (Araceae)

A vigorous perennial herb growing up to 6 feet tall, composed of many long, slender, grass-like leaves up to ¾-inch wide rising from a horizontal rootstock. The flowers are minute and greenish-yellow in color, occurring on a 4-inch long spike resembling a finger. The fruit is berry-like. Native to eastern North America, Europe and Asia.

Cultivation and Propagation: Calamus is hardy throughout the U.S. and much of Canada. It thrives best in a rich soil, but can be grown in shallow water on dry land. It is propagated by division of the rootstock in spring or fall. Pieces of the rhizome should be planted horizontally, an inch or two deep, a foot apart in each direction, with the leaf-shoots upward. They can be planted in marshes and at the edges of ponds and streams. They will do well in the garden if the soil is rich and is kept moist by frequent waterings. Formerly it was maintained that calamus would not flower unless its roots were submerged in water. This author, however, has seen many exceptions to this belief.

Harvesting: The rhizomes should be collected when 2–3 years old, in early spring before new growth, or in the late autumn. The leaves and rootlets should be removed and the rhizomes washed thoroughly. They should be dried without the application of heat. Upon drying, the rhizomes lose 70 to 75 percent of their weight, but improve in flavor and aroma. They should be stored in a cool dry place, as calamus deteriorates with age, heat and moisture. Also dried roots are often eaten by worms or small boring beetles. After a year or so of storage the roots have lost much of their active principle.

CALIFORNIA POPPY

Eschscholzia californica Cham.;
Poppy family (Papaveraceae)

A perennial herb to 2 feet tall (usually less in the wild) with bluish-green, finely-divided leaves. The flowers open in the sunshine, are up to 4 inches across, and are on long stalks. On wild plants, the flowers are 4-petaled and orange-yellow, but there are many horticultural varieties. It blooms from July 1st to October the first year, and again each April in areas where it grows as a perennial. The fruit is a thin, ribbed capsule 3–4 inches long. Native to California and Oregon; naturalized in Europe.

Cultivation and Propagation: The California poppy is grown as an annual in cold-winter areas, and as a perennial in California and the South. The seeds should be sown where the plants are to stand, as they don't transplant well. They should be sown as early as weather permits. The plants like a sunny exposure and do well on hillsides and dry, rocky places. In the garden, the seedlings should be thinned so that the plants will stand 6–8 inches apart. They stand considerable cold and will continue to bloom after the first frosts. In cold areas, if the roots are protected, the plant will live over winter and bloom the following spring.

Harvesting: The outer leaves may be picked and dried at any time. The flowers may be removed and seed capsules may be picked when unripe and dried with the leaves. In autumn the plants should be cut off at the ground and dried before they begin to wilt from the cold.

Note: The California poppy is the state flower of California and is protected by a state law which provides stiff fines for people caught picking or mutilating it. This law is not to keep people from getting high. It is to protect the poppy, which is rapidly becoming wiped out by road construction and land development.

The seeds are cheap and the plant easy to grow. If you plan on using this poppy, please grow your own. Home-grown poppies are not subject to the law.

CATNIP
Nepeta cataria L.; Mint family (Labiatae)

A hardy, upright, perennial herb with sturdy stems bearing hairy, heart-shaped, grayish-green leaves. The flowers are white or lilac, ¼-inch long, and occur in several clusters toward the tips of the branches. Native of Eurasia, naturalized in North America.

Cultivation and Propagation: It is easily cultivated in any garden soil, with little care, as the plant does not require the moisture that most mint plants need. Plants should be grown from seed sown where they are going to stand. Bruised or recently transplanted plants are likely to be eaten by cats unless protected. The seed should be sown very thinly in rows 20 inches apart and the seedlings thinned out to 20 inches apart in the rows. It requires almost no care except occasional weeding. A bed will last several years. It can also be propagated by division of the roots in spring.

Harvesting: The herb is harvested just before flowering in middle to late summer on a dry sunny day and in late morning when all dew is gone. Drying should be done carefully. The leaves are stripped from the stems and dried as quickly as possible with good ventilation out of direct sunlight, or in an oven at 150°F to avoid losing much volatile oil.

CHICALOTE; PRICKLY POPPY

Argemone mexicana L.; Poppy family (Papaveraceae)

An annual herb 1 to 3 feet high with prickly stems, leaves and capsules. The flowers are yellow or orange, up to 2½ inches across, and followed by an oblong seed capsule. The leaves are white-veined and 4 to 6 inches long. Native to tropical America but naturalized in the southeastern U.S.

Cultivation and Propagation: Although generally grown as an annual, this poppy is sometimes a biennial or perennial. It prefers a light soil but it will do well in most soils if given a full sunny exposure. It is propagated by seeds sown in early spring. The seedlings, like most poppies, dislike transplanting, so the seeds are usually sown where they are to stand. However, they may be sown in pots and, if replanted outside without disturbing the roots, they will do well. It blooms in late summer and reseeds itself readily.

Harvesting: The unripe capsules may be incised in the same manner as opium poppies and an opium-like substitute obtained. However, the stout prickles which cover the capsule make this difficult. The seed may be harvested by keeping a close watch on the capsules and removing them when they first begin to open, before the seeds spill out.

COLEUS
Mint family (Labiatae)

Two species of *Coleus* are used as hallucinogens; both are cultivated in the U.S. They are:

Coleus blumei Benth. This is the common cultivated coleus. A tender perennial herb usually not exceeding 3 feet in height. The leaves are ovate, pointed, 4 inches or more long, edged with rounded teeth. They are mottled with red, green, yellow and purple. The flowers are dark blue or whitish, in a terminal spike. Native to Java. Naturalized throughout the tropics. A common house plant in the U.S.

C. pumilus. A low herb with lax stems which lie on the ground and root at the lower joints, or hang over the sides of the pot. The leaves are smaller than those of *C. blumei,* usually not exceeding 2 inches long. The flowers are in long racemes. Native to the Philippines.

Cultivation and Propagation: Coleus does best in strong, indirect light in a warm, rich, loose, well-drained soil with ample water.

Coleus seeds should be started indoors in flats of fine soil covered with a pan of glass or a sheet of plastic wrap. The seeds should be sown thinly and covered with a thin layer of soil. With bottom heat they will come up within 2 weeks. When large enough to handle, the seedlings should be transplanted to pots. When all danger of frost is past the plants may be set out in the garden.

Few plants root more easily than coleus. Cuttings may be taken at any time of the year and rooted in shallow water.

Coleus plants should be fed regularly with a high nitrogen fertilizer to stimulate foliage growth. Mealybugs and aphids are its worst enemies; slugs and snails attack it in the garden.

Harvesting: All parts of the plant are psychoactive, but only the leaves and flowering tops should be used, as new leaves will grow to replace them. Flowering tops should be picked off before they seed, as they seriously sap the energy of the rest of the plant. These may be stored in the freezer along with fresh leaves that have fallen off until there are enough for a dose. Dried leaves do not seem to have any effect. When picking fresh leaves it is best to remove the lower leaves and take cuttings from the branch tips. Some leaves should be left on the base of the plant to give it energy to send out new shoots.

COLORINES
Erythrina flabelliformis Kearny;
Bean family (Leguminosae)

A shrub or small tree growing up to 10 feet high with spiny branches and leaves composed of fan-shaped leaflets. The flowers are bright scarlet, in short crowded racemes. The pods are up to 1 foot long, containing bright scarlet oval seeds. Native to southern Arizona, New Mexico, and Mexico.

Cultivation and Propapagation: This erythrina may be grown outside in California and Florida, but must be grown in the greenhouse in cold-winter areas. It prefers a well-drained soil and full sun, and likes frequent waterings but will stand considerable drought.

Propagated by seeds which need nicking and soaking, and by cuttings of growing wood.

Harvesting: When the ripe pods begin to open in the fall they may be gathered and the seeds removed.

DAMIANA
Turnera diffusa; Turnera family (Turneraceae)

A small shrub with smooth inch-long, pale green leaves which have dense hairs on the underside. The flowers are yellow, rising from the leaf axils, followed by a one-celled capsule, which splits into 3 pieces. Native to the Southwest and Mexico.

Cultivation and Propagation: Damiana may be planted outdoors in the South and West, or in the greenhouse in the North. It thrives in any good soil if given a sunny location. It should be watered freely from spring to fall, and sparingly in winter. In the greenhouse the temperature should stand around 55° at night. Damiana is propagated by seeds and cuttings.

Harvesting: The leaves and tops are harvested while the plant is in flower. As some of the active principle is volatile, the tops are preferably dried in the shade, without the application of heat.

DATURAS
Nightside family (Solanaceae)

This genus has 15 to 20 species ranging from annual and perennial herbs to shrubs and trees, with trumpet-shaped flowers. All of these are hallucinogenic.

Herbaceous Daturas

Datura fastuosa L., formerly *D. metel.* An annual herb, 4 to 5 feet tall, with ovate 7- to 8-inch leaves. The flower is 7 inches long, white inside, violet and yellowish outside, with a purple calyx. The fruit is a 1¼-inch-diameter spiny capsule. There are also double-flowered and blue-, red-, and yellow-flowered varieties. Native to India and naturalized in the tropics of both hemispheres.

D. inoxia Mill. A low-growing, spreading perennial with hairy 2- to 4-inch leaves. The flowers are white, 6 to 7 inches long, 10-lobed. The fruit is spiny, 2 inches or more in diameter. Native to Mexico and the Southwest. Similar to *D. meteloides*. The seeds take up to several weeks to germinate. Cultivated as an annual in the North.

D. meteloides DC. An erect perennial herb with 2- to 5-inch leaves. The flowers are white, 8 inches long, often tinged with rose or violet, fragrant. The capsule is intensely spiny, 2 inches in diameter. Native to the Southwest and Mexico. The seeds take 3 to 5 weeks to sprout and should be started in damp peat moss. Do not pre-soak the seeds. Plants should be spaced 3 to 4 feet apart. Cultivated as an annual in the North.

D. stramonium L. "Jimson weed." A green-stemmed, hairless annual, 2 to 4 feet tall, with few branches and 2- 8-inch-long ovate leaves. The flowers are white, 4 inches long. The capsule is egg-shaped, to 2 inches long, filled with many black seeds. In *D. Stramonium* var. *tatula* the flower is violet-purple or lavender; the stems are purple. Naturalized throughout the world. They are easily grown from seeds, which sprout quickly even without bottom heat. Does well in rich soil in a dry, sunny location. May be sown in the open in May in mounds 18 inches apart with four seeds in each mound. Thin out all but the healthiest plant after sprouting.

D. chlorantha Hook. A hairless, perennial shrub, occasionally reaching 10 feet tall, with almost triangular, wavy-margined leaves. The flowers are yellow, drooping, followed by a prickly capsule. This is not a true tree datura although it occasionally reaches similar heights. Generally grown as a tall annual.

Cultivation and Propagation: The herbaceous daturas are generally grown from seeds in early spring.

They should be started in flats indoors in the North, or where they are to stand in warmer areas. The perennial kinds usually rise from thick tuberous roots. In the North these may be dug in autumn and stored in semi-dry peat moss, sawdust, or sand in a cool place until spring. These daturas generally prefer loose, sandy soils, somewhat on the dry side, and a sunny location. Those native to the Southwest will stand considerable drought.

Harvesting: The leaves and tops are preferably harvested when the plants are in full bloom, but they may be gathered at any time from the appearance of flowers until frost. They should be stripped from the stem and dried as quickly as possible. Fresh leaves have a fetid odor, which is lost on drying. Seeds harvested for psychoactive purposes are collected by removing the capsules when they are ripe, but are still green and unopened. These are dried in the sun or by low heat. Seeds for growing purposes should be gathered by collecting capsules that are just opening, removing the seeds and drying in the sun.

Tree Daturas

Datura arborea L. A small tree, growing to 10 feet tall with 8-inch-long soft hairy leaves in pairs. The margins are smooth and never wavy. The flowers are musky-scented, white, veined with green, 6 to 9 inches long, and hanging. The calyx splits down one side. The fruit is spineless, 2½ inches long. Native to Peru and Chile. May be distinguished from *D. candida* by the length of the flowers and leaves.

D.candida (Pers.) Pasq. A small tree growing 10 to 12 feet tall with 16-inch-long, ovate, downy leaves. The flowers are white, musky-scented, hanging, and about 10 inches long. The calyx splits down one side. The fruit is smooth, 2½ inches long. Native to tropical America. May be distinguished from *D. arborea* by the extreme length of the leaves and from *D. suaveolens* by the calyx and the leaves. Cuttings root slowly.

D. suaveolens Humb. & Bonpl. A small tree, 10 to 15 feet high , with ovate 6- to 12-inch-long leaves, only slightly hairy. The flowers are white-nerved with green, hanging, 9 to 12 inches long. The calyx is inflated, with 5 obscure teeth. The fruit is smooth, spindle-shaped, 5 inches long. Native to Brazil. May be distinguished from *D. arborea* and *D. candida* by the 5-toothed calyx.

D. sanguinea Kuiz. & Par. "Huanto." A small tree, 4 to 12 feet tall, with 7-inch-long ovate leaves, shining green on the upper side. The flowers are 8 to 10 inches long, drooping, brilliant orange-red with yellow veins, not fragrant. The fruit is top-shaped, spineless, 3½ inches long. Native to Peru. Distinguished from all others by the red flowers. Rare; cuttings are almost impossible to take. Prefers cool areas.

Cultivation and Propagation: The tree daturas may be grown outdoors in California and the South or as tub plants in the North. They may be propagated by seed when available. Bottom heat greatly speeds up germination. Young plants should be watered frequently until tub-plant size. They need a rich, well-drained soil and a large tub. A large root-system is required for good bloom. In the summer they should be watered once a week with liquid fertilizer. In cold-winter areas, tub plants may be kept outdoors in summer and wintered-over in a cellar or similar place, as they require little moisture and light while dormant. When planted outdoors they should be sheltered from wind. Except for *D. sanguinea*, they may also be propagated by cuttings taken with heels, which root easily in water. *D. sanguinea* is the hardiest of the four.

Harvesting: The leaves may be harvested at any time, but you should leave enough for good growth. Most rarely set seed; when they do, the capsules should be gathered when ripe, and the seeds dried in the sun.

DOÑANA
Coryphantha macromeris (Engl.) Lem.; Cactus family
(Cactaceae)

A low cylindrical cactus to 8 inches tall, branching at the base, covered with several inch-long, soft, spine-tipped tubercles. The flowers are purple, 5 inches across. Native to Mexico and West Texas.

Cultivation and Propagation: Doñana may be grown outdoors in the West and South or as a pot plant in the North. It may be cultivated in the same manner as San Pedro except that it is thinner-skinned and more subject to mealy-bugs and scale insects. Doñana also makes small offsets at the end of the lower tubercles. When these reach the size of a nickel they may be removed and rooted.

Harvesting: Always leave a part of the plant with several tubercles intact so that it may grow new plants.

To reduce bulk, cactus material may be sliced thinly and dried quickly in the sun or at a low heat.

FENNEL
Foeniculum vulgare Mill;
Carrot family (Umbelliferae)

A perennial herb growing to 5 feet high, with blue-green stems and leaves. The leaves are finely divided into threadlike leaflets. The flower cluster is a large umbel, composed of 15 to 20 yellow flowers. Native of southern Europe; naturalized in western U.S.

Cultivation and Propagation: Fennel is grown as an annual or biennial in cold-winter areas. Grow in a light, well-drained soil in full sun. The seed should be sown in early spring where the plants are to stand, and the seedlings thinned to 1 foot apart.

Harvesting: The ripe seeds are the source of the psychotropic oil. These should be gathered when they are dry and have turned a yellowish-brown color. The young leaves may be used in salads and fish dishes. Older leaves are fragrant but tough.

HAWAIIAN BABY WOODROSE
Argyreia nervosa Bojer.;
Morning Glory family (Convolvulaceae)

A large perennial climbing vine with heart-shaped leaves up to 1 foot across, backed with silvery hairs. The flowers are 2 to 3 inches long, rose-colored, on

6-inch stalks. Pods dry to a smooth, dark brown, filbert-sized capsule containing 1 to 4 furry brown seeds. The capsule is surrounded by a dry calyx divided into 5 petal-like sections. Native to Asia; naturalized and cultivated in Hawaii.

Cultivation and Propagation: It may be grown outdoors in southern California and Florida. Elsewhere it should be grown in a large pot or tub outdoors in the summer, brought indoors in winter. It may be propagated by cuttings or seeds, and in the spring by division. The seed may be sprouted by making a small nick in the seedcoat away from the germ eye. Soak the seed until it swells. Plant ½-inch deep in loose rich soil. Do not use bottom heat. After the cotyledons appear, water sparingly, letting the soil surface dry out to a depth of ½-inch. Over-watering casues stem and root rot. The plant grows slowly until it develops a half-dozen leaves; after this it grows quickly. In its first year this plant grows into a small bush 1 to 2 feet tall. During this time it may be grown in a large pot and kept indoors in winter. The next spring it will grow into a very large vine and should produce flowers and seeds. In this second year it should be planted out, or grown in a tub. In cold-winter areas the roots should be lifted and stored or the tub kept in a cool place until spring.

The methods of increasing the alkaloid content of morning glories (which see) may be applied to this vine.

Harvesting: The seed pods should be harvested when thoroughly dry. They should be stored in a cool, dry place. Their potency may begin to decrease after 6–9 months.

HAWAIIAN WOODROSE
Merremia tuberosa;
Morning Glory family (Convolvulaceae)

A slender perennial vine with leaves divided into 5 to 7 narrow lobes. The flowers are yellow, followed by a smooth round capsule, surrounded by 5 petal-like sepals. Native to Asia; naturalized and cultivated in Hawaii.

Cultivation and Propagation: The large woodrose may be grown outdoors in southern California and the South. The seed of the large woodrose must be nicked well before it will grow. Cut a nick in the seedcoat with a hacksaw, or cut the small end of the seed off. Soak for 24 hours or until it swells. Then place the seed in a bowl or cup of damp peat moss, cover it with plastic wrap, and put it over the pilot light of your stove, or anywhere that maintains a temperature of 80°F or more. Ordinary bottom heat usually isn't warm enough. Check every few days until it sprouts in 4 to 10 days. Once sprouted, plant in a 3- to 4-inch pot if grown indoors, or start seed in May if to be grown outdoors. Place the pot in a large sunny window and give the vine something to twine around. I have seen these vines grow one foot or more per week. It is very easy to grow after sprouting. It can take little or much watering and much abuse. The vine will flower the second and subsequent years.

Harvesting: The pods may be harvested when they are thoroughly dry. Its storage properties are the same as those of the baby woodrose.

HELIOTROPE
Valeriana officinalis L.;
Valerian family (Valerianaceae)

Perennial herb 2–5 feet high with pinnately divided leaves and clusters of small, whitish, pinkish, or lavender flowers. Very fragrant. Native of Europe and N. Asia; naturalized in North America.

Cultivation and Propagation: It is easily grown from seed sown $^1/_{16}$ inch deep in light, sandy soil. It may be propagated by division of the rootstock in spring. It spreads itself rapidly by suckers rising from the roots.

Harvesting: Flowering tops should be cut off to make the roots develop more. In September or October the tops should be cut completely and the large root crowns dug, washed, and dried.

HENBANE
Hyoscyamus niger L.;
Nightshade family (Solanaceae)

An annual or biennial herb, to 2½ feet high, with hairy, 3- to 8-inch-long leaves. The flowers are 1 inch across, greenish-yellow with purple veins; they grow in spikes from June to September. The seed capsule is filled with many pitted seeds. Naturalized infrequently across southern Canada and the northern U.S.

Cultivation and Propagation: Henbane does well in most soils, as it is found wild in dry waste places. It is propagated easily by seed. Henbane seed is very viable. I have sprouted seeds collected from a capsule on a plant that had gone through a winter's rain and hard frost and had almost deteriorated away, and got 90 percent germination. The seed should be planted in May or when the weather is in the 70's. It should be sown very thinly in rows 2 to 3 feet apart. The bed should be kept moist until sprouting, and the seedlings should be thinned to 1½ to 2 feet apart in the row. They may also be sown in flats at room temperature and transplanted out on a cool day. Henbane is sometimes attacked by potato pests and will occasionally mildew like tomato plants.

Harvesting: Henbane leaves and tops should be collected when the plant is in full flower. This is usually in June, July, or sometimes August. The leaves should be dried quickly in the sun, as it will lose its properties if kept in a damp state too long. The herb will lose approximately 80 percent of its weight in drying. Fresh henbane leaves have a fetid ordor when handled, which they lose upon drying. The seed is up to ten times as strong as the leaves. The capsules may be gathered in August, before they open. The seeds are shaken out and dried in the sun if to be used for growing purposes, or dried quickly at a low heat if to be used psychoactively.

HOPS

Humulus lupulus L.; Hemp family (Cannabinaceae)

A perennial twining vine growing from 15 to 30 feet long with oval 3- to 5-lobed leaves having coarsely-toothed edges. Male and female flowers occur on separate plants. Native to Eurasia.

Cultivation and Propagation: Seed Propagation:
Hops seed is the type of seed with a dormant embryo, as many tree and wild plant seeds have. Many people's failure to sprout hops seed is due not to the unviability of the seed, but to the fact that they have taken no steps to break the dormancy of the embryo before sowing.

To break this dormancy, first place your seeds in a glass of water. You will notice that most of the seeds will float and a few will sink. The seeds which float are viable and should be skimmed off and placed in another container of water. The material which sinks should be discarded, as it consists of broken seeds, dead material, and other debris. Soak the floating seeds for 24 to 40 hours. During this time many of the seeds will sink. Take all of the seeds and mix them with damp peat moss in a plastic sandwich bag. Close and seal it and place it in your refrigerator for 5 to 6 weeks. At the end of this time take the bag out and keep it at room temperature. The peat moss may be placed in a shallow container covered with plastic wrap. Sift through the peat moss–seed mixture every day, looking for sprouted seed. Do not let the peat moss dry out. The seeds can germinate each day for 10 to 21 days. A few may sprout as late as 4 weeks. The sprouts should be removed and planted root down in loose, rich, well-drained soil. From germination until a few true leaves form, hops sprouts are very sensitive to overwatering. Keep the soil slightly on the dry side. While the peat moss is in the refrigerator and afterwards, you may notice some white mold forming. Don't worry about this. It only feeds on dead matter, not on viable seeds. When storing seeds, keep from moisture and heat, as these destroy viability. I know of only one source of viable hops seeds: the Redwood City Seed Company (see *Sources*). The above method of germination was developed by this company and has been reprinted by its kind permission.

Rhizome Cultivation: Hops are propagated worldwide by rhizomes, but are rarely available to the general public as a result of the U.S. federal government's attempts to stop their possible abuse as material grafted onto marijuana stocks. However, they are still available from Wine and the People (see *Sources*). Propagating hops by rhizomes has the advantage over seeds in that they will sprout sooner after planting if the weather is warm. However, they have serious disadvantages. Propagation by cuttings for too long limits the genetic bank of the plant. Thus the plant eventually ceases to produce seed and comes to an evolutionary dead end, because without seed natural mutations cannot occur. The plant then becomes totally dependent on man for its survival. All of the hops grown commercially in this country are seedless hybrids (all polyploid hops are sterile). Hybrid plants are often more susceptible to disease, although more vigorous growing than ordinary plants. Molds, viruses and insects that attack hops plants continue to mutate and evolve stronger strains freely, while seedless hops are not able to mutate resistant strains, thus decreasing the survival potential of the hybrid. With the standardization of the beer-making industry across the world, the last remaining areas that grow seeded hops are rapidly being forced to grow only seedless hybrids. If you wish to use roots, the cuttings should be planted horizontally with the buds upwards, 2 inches deep in a well-worked, rich loamy soil. Hops may also be propagated by layering. The lower part of the vine is laid on the ground and covered with soil. This will root and may be used for cuttings in winter. Hops is also propagated by cuttings of the shoots and branches. Each hops plant should be given a space 18 feet tall to climb.

Harvesting: When harvesting hops that has been grafted to hemp, the whole plant may be used. The cones should be harvested when ripe in late July or early August. They should be dried quickly, soon after harvesting, in the sun or in the oven at a low heat (140°–160°F). If this is not done they will deteriorate rapidly after picking. When harvesting hops that have been grafted to cannabis, both cones and leaves may be used. The same drying rules apply to these.

HYDRANGEA

Hydrangea paniculata Sieb. var. *grandiflora;*
Saxifrage family (Saxifragaceae)

This is the commonest hardy hydrangea in cultivation. It is a tree-like shrub 8 to 30 feet high, with 3–5-inch-long oval leaves. The flowers are whitish, in dense clusters 8 to 15 inches long. The flowers sometimes change to pink and purple with age. Native to China and Japan. A common garden plant in the U.S.

Cultivation and Propagation: Hardy everywhere except north central U.S. (Montana, North Dakota, and Minnesota), but can be grown in sheltered places there. Hydrangeas bloom best in full sun, but will do well in partial shade.

They are best propagated by cuttings of green growth in June. The cuttings should be the ends of nonflowering shoots and should have 2–3 pairs of leaves. The bottom pair of leaves should be removed and the stem cut just below a joint. They should be placed in moist sand in a shady place.

Seeds are uncommon but when available should be sown in a sandy, peaty soil in spring in a greenhouse or sheltered place.

Hydrangeas can be transplanted easily. The color of the blossoms may be altered by the addition of certain minerals to the soil. Special solutions for this purpose are available at many nurseries.

Harvesting: Leaves can be harvested at any time. A single small bush will provide large quantities of leaves and flowers when pruned in the fall.

IOCHROMA
Nightshade family (Solanaceae)

Iochroma is a genus of tropical shrubs or small trees with tubular flowers, several species of which are cultivated in the U.S.

Iochroma coccineum Schow. A shrub with hairy branches and oblong leaves. The flowers are 2 inches long, scarlet, and in drooping clusters. Native to Central America.

I. fuchsioides Miers. A shrub with narrow, almost hairless leaves, and 1½-long orange-scarlet flowers in drooping clusters. Native to Peru.

I. lanceolatum Miers. A shrub growing to 8 feet tall with hairy, ovate to narrow leaves. The flowers are 2 inches long, purple-blue. Native to Ecuador.

I. tubulosum Benth. A hairy shrub, 6 to 8 feet high, with ovate leaves and deep blue 1½-inch-long flowers in drooping clusters. Native to Colombia.

Cultivation and Propagation: Iochroma may be grown outdoors in California and the South, but must be grown indoors in the North. Propagated by seeds when available; or by cuttings, preferably taken in February or early March. Cuttings take several weeks to root.

Harvesting: Leaves may be picked and dried any time there is sufficient growth to replace them. Harvesting should be stopped in the winter when growth is slow or halted. Flowers may be dried as they begin to wilt.

KAVA KAVA

Piper methysticum Forst.; Pepper family (Piperaceae)

A perennial, soft-wooded shrub growing 8 to 10 feet tall, with 8-inch ovate to heart-shaped leaves. The flower spikes are opposite the leaves; male and female flowers occur on separate plants. Native to the Pacific Islands.

Cultivation and Propagation: In the Pacific Islands kava does best in the cool, moist highlands up to 1000 feet above sea level where the daytime summer temperatures are between 80° and 90°. It may be grown in southern Florida, but elsewhere it requires greenhouse temperatures. It prefers a loose, rich soil with good drainage and frequent watering. It does well on stony ground. The best crops are grown on virgin soil. If two consecutive crops are raised on the same soil the second crop will be poor. The plant rarely produces seeds and is generally propagated by cuttings of the firm wood. These are susceptible to fungus diseases because of the high humidity the plant requires. Plants should be spaced about 6 feet apart either way. This furnishes about 1200 plants per acre. Kava makes a good house plant.

Harvesting: The main rootstock begins just below the surface of the ground and continues for two feet or more. It gets to be 3–5 inches thick after 2½–4 years growth, and may weigh 12–16 lb. From it radiate many tough roots. Rootstocks usually reach maximum growth at about 6 years, but the older the plant the more potent it will be. These may be dug and used fresh or dried in the sun. The lower stems are also active. Before drying, the rootstocks and lower stems should be scraped of their outer coating and cut into pieces weighing ½–1½ oz. each. Drying reduces weight to about ⅕. The tough radiating roots may be dug and used fresh at any time but the plant should be given time to generate new roots.

For further information on the botany, chemistry, history and uses of kava see *Kava Kava: The Famous Drug Plant of the South Sea Islands,* by Dr. E. F. Steinmetz, also published by the Twentieth Century Alchemist.

KHAT
Catha edulis Forsk.;
Burning Bush family (Celastreae)

An evergreen shrub or tree to 10 feet tall, with oval, 4-inch-long leaves. The flowers are small, white, and

5-petaled. The fruit is an oblong 3-angled capsule containing 1 to 3 seeds. Native from Abyssinia to South Africa.

Cultivation and Propagation: Khat may be grown outdoors in Florida and California, and as a greenhouse plant in the North. It needs fast drainage and does poorly in a rich moist soil. Does best in hot areas in poor dry soil. Propagated by cuttings taken in spring or, more effectively, by layering. Khat rarely sets seed in this country. It should be pinched or pruned to keep it compact, and to produce more buds.

Harvesting: The buds, branch tips and young leaves from pruning may be used fresh or dried. Do not harvest too often or cut the branch tips too far back, as this may destroy active buds and destroy new growth.

LION'S TAIL
Leonotis leonurus R. Br.; Mint family (Labiatae)

A shrubby, branching perennial 3 to 6 feet high with 2- to 5-inch-long hairy-toothed leaves. The tubular flowers are 2 inches long, bright red, yellow, or orange-red, and bloom in late spring and autumn. Native to Africa.

Cultivation and Propagation: *Leonotis* may be planted outdoors in California and the South; it may be grown as an annual in the North, or brought into the greenhouse during winter. It should be planted in full sun, as it will not flower in the shade. It prefers a dry soil and is drought-resistant. Water deeply and infrequently.

Leonotis may be propagated by seeds sown indoors from January to February. Cuttings root easily at any time of the year. For good-sized plants, cuttings should be taken in the early spring.

Harvesting: The leaves and flowers are smoked for their cannabis-like effects. These parts may be gathered at any time and dried quickly. Harvest no more than one-third of the leaves at one time. Let the plant grow and fill out for at least a month before harvesting again. In Africa a resin is gathered from the leaves. Plants grown in less torrid climates do not tend to exude this resin. Such leaves can be smoked, however, or subjected to alcohol extraction.

LOBELIA
Lobelia inflata L.; Lobelia family (Lobeliaceae)

An herbaceous annual growing to 3 feet high with hairy, ovate leaves. The flowers are ¼-inch long, light blue or whitish, followed by an inflated seed capsule. Native from Labrador south to Georgia and Arkansas.

Cultivation and Propagation: Lobelia is best propagated from seed sown in January or early February in flats of fine soil. The seeds are very small, and difficult to sow thinly enough. They may be mixed with fine sand or with herbal (non-viable) seed. The seedlings should be transplanted to pots when large enough to handle, and set outdoors in early June. It will do well in ordinary garden soil if given a cool, shady location. In hot areas it will stop flowering in mid-summer. Plants may be lifted in fall, kept over winter, and new plants started from cuttings of these taken in January or February.

Harvesting: The leaves and tops should be harvested in August and September. The seeds are the most potent part of the plant. These should be gathered when the capsules ripen.

MADAGASCAR PERIWINKLE
Catharanthus rosea Don.;
Dogbane family (Apocynaceae)

Formerly *Vinca rosea.* A tender erect perennial with oblong leaves, growing to two feet tall. It is ever-blooming. The flowers are rosy purple or white, 1½ inches across. Origin unknown; now naturalized in the tropics of every continent.

Cultivation and Propagation: Madagascar periwinkle may be grown as a tender perennial in California and Florida or cultivated as an annual elsewhere. The seed should be sown thinly from January to March in flats of sandy soil and kept at a temperature of 65° to 70°F. When the seedlings show the second leaf they should be thinned out to a distance of about 1 inch apart. When they have 5 or 6 leaves they should be potted in 2-inch pots. When all danger of frost is over, they may be set out a foot apart each way.

Catharanthus prefers a light sandy loam, and will not do well in a very heavy soil. When watering, the soil should be well soaked and then left alone for several days. It does well in semi-shady situations.

A few plants may be lifted in the fall and carried over winter in pots. Cuttings from these may be used for propagation.

Harvesting: Leaves and flowers may be gathered any time after the plant begins to flower. In fall the plants should be cut off at the ground and dried quickly, before cold weather starts them wilting.

MANDRAGORE; MANDRAKE
Mandragora officinarum L.;
Nightshade family (Solanaceae)

A stemless herbaceous perennial with ovate foot-long leaves rising directly from the root. The flowers are 1 inch long, purple or greenish yellow, followed by an oblong greenish berry. Native of southern Europe.

Cultivation and Propagation: The mandragore is hardy throughout the U.S. It likes a light, deep soil, as the roots run far down. They will do poorly in a soil that is chalky or excessively gravelly. If the soil is too wet in winter, the roots will rot. It is propagated from seeds which should be sown in deep flats or, better, singly in pots. These should be kept well-watered and when they reach a good size they should be carefully set out at least 2 feet apart.

Harvesting: The roots should be dug after the second or third year. If left in the ground they will grow to a great age, and will have large branching roots up to four feet long.

Note: Do not confuse this Old World mandrake with the American mandrake *(Podophyllum peltatum)* whose roots are sold by many herb companies under the name "Mandrake roots." These roots are a powerful cathartic poison. The plants are unmistakably different.

MARABA

Kaempferia galanga L.;
Ginger family (Zingiberaceae)

A stemless perennial herb with 6-inch-long leaves rising directly from the rootstock. The flowers are white with a violet spot. Native to New Guinea.

Cultivation and Propagation: *Kaempferia* will not endure frost. It may be grown in the open in the South if well protected. In the rest of the country it should be grown indoors in a large pot of rich soil. Once the roots have developed it should be given plenty of water. The pots may be kept in water half their depth. It should be fed occasionally with liquid fertilizer. Towards the end of summer the amount of water should be gradually lessened. The roots should be kept almost dry during winter. In the spring the roots may be divided to form new plants.

Harvesting: In spring, when dividing the roots, some of them may be split open and dried quickly without heat, or used fresh.

MATÉ

Ilex paraguayensis St. Hil.;
Holly family (Aquifoliaceae)

An evergreen shrub or small tree growing to 20 feet tall, with oval, wavy-toothed leaves. The flowers are tiny and white, followed by red or reddish-brown berries. Native to Brazil.

Cultivation and Propagation: This ilex will do well in a rich, well-drained soil. It grows very rapidly and can produce a crop after one year's growth from seed. The seed, however, must be stratified, as it does not germinate until the second year. Seedlings should be transplanted in early fall or in the spring, before new growth starts. Some of the leaves should be stripped off first to lessen the shock. It may also be propagated by cuttings under glass.

Harvesting: The branch tips bearing young leaves should be cut when the growth is new. These should be lightly toasted in an oven until dry, and the twigs removed and discarded.

MESCAL BEANS
Sophora secundiflora (Orteg) Lag.;
Bean family (Leguminosae)

A small tree reaching 35 feet with age, with 4- to 6-inch leaves divided into 7 to 9 leaflets. The flowers are violet-blue, very fragrant, and occur in clusters up to 8 inches long; they bloom from February to April. The pod is furry and contains up to 8 red seeds. Native to Texas and New Mexico.

Cultivation and Propagation: It can be grown outside in California and the South, or may be grown as a tub plant in the North, and brought inside during the cold months. It grows slowly in cool-summer regions. It thrives in hot sun and a well-drained, alkaline soil. The soil should be kept on the dryish side except when blooming. It is propagated from seeds, which should be nicked and soaked, or from greenwood cuttings and layers.

Harvesting: In the fall the pods will open, exposing the seeds, which should be removed and stored immediately, before children can get to them.

MORMON TEA
Ephedra nevadensis Wats.;
Gnetum family (Gnetaceae)

An erect, broom-like shrub 2 feet high. The leafless stems are pale green when young and olive brown with age. Male and female flowers are found on separate plants. The seeds are a smooth brown color and paired. Common on slopes and hills, mostly below 4,500 feet elevation. Native to the Mohave and Colorado deserts, east to Utah, Arizona, and New Mexico.

Cultivation and Propagation: Ephedra should be planted in dry locations. It thrives in ordinary loamy soil and does very well in a loose rocky soil with full sun and little water. It is most often propagated by division of the clumps in spring, and seeds sown in a light sandy soil in early spring. It may also be propagated by layers and suckers. It makes an excellent ground cover on rocky slopes.

Harvesting: The tops of the branches may be picked and dried at any time as long as the plant is not denuded or the branches cut back past the viable buds.

MORNING GLORY
Ipomoea sp.; Morning Glory family (Convolvulaceae)

This species is often called *I. violacea,* but it is my contention that it is properly *I. tricolor.* It is a perennial twining vine, growing from 10 to 20 feet high, with heart-shaped leaves to 5 inches long. The flowers are funnel-shaped, purplish blue with a white tube. Native to tropical America. Psychoactive varieties are Heavenly Blue, Pearly Gates, Flying Saucers, Wedding Bells, Blue Star, and Summer Skies.

Cultivation and Propagation: Although this species is a perennial it is usually cultivated as an annual in this country. Morning glories thrive in a strong, well-drained soil in a sunny site with plenty of water, but they will do well almost anywhere. The seeds have a hard seedcoat and should be nicked or soaked 2 hours in warm water before sowing. If the seeds are nicked and soaked, the vines will generally flower 6 weeks after sowing. The seeds should be planted ¼–½ inch deep and not less than 6 inches apart. This species tends to run to vine unless the roots are cramped. This may be done by standing the vines in pots and allowing them to become slightly potbound before setting them out. Although morning glories like a lot of water, if the roots are kept damp constantly, the vines will produce few flowers and they will set very little seed. Various methods have been devised to increase the alkaloid content of the seeds by altering the soil chemistry and using hormones. An interesting account of these methods is found in the book *Home Grown Highs* by Mary Jane Superweed.

Harvesting: The seeds may be gathered as the pods become brown and dry. Immature seeds are more bitter than ripe ones. It has been reported that immature seeds contain more alkaloids, but this has not been confirmed. There are approximately 850 seeds per ounce of the Heavenly Blue variety. The stem and leaves contain some alkaloid. However, because they contain purgative principles, this part of the plant is used only in extraction. If used, pick fresh and dry quickly without heat.

Note: Some suppliers coat their seeds with toxins either as a fungicide or to discourage their use as hallucinogens. The symptoms of ingesting treated seeds are vomiting and diarrhea. Some people experience nausea from ingesting untreated seeds and fear they have taken treated seeds. However, if the company has treated their seeds, they must say so on the package. To test your susceptibility to nausea, chew 50 to 100 seeds or less the first time.

NUTMEG
Myristica fragrans Houtt.;
Nutmeg family (Myristicaceae)

A tree growing to 70 feet tall with oblong, brownish, 5-inch leaves. The flowers are small, with male and female borne on separate trees. The fruit is reddish to yellowish, splitting into 2 valves. The brown seed (nutmeg) is surrounded by a scarlet aril (mace). Native to the East Indies; cultivated in the West Indies and South America.

Cultivation and Propagation: The nutmeg tree thrives in a hot, moist climate, in a well-drained soil with partial shade. It may be grown outdoors in southern Florida. Elsewhere it should be planted in a greenhouse with relatively high humidity. It requires a moist soil, but should not be kept wet, as the roots will rot. To obtain nutmegs both sexes should be planted. One male is sufficient to pollinate 10 to 12 females. When grown from seed, they should be planted singly in pots, and transplanted when 8 to 10 inches high. The trees will begin to bear in 7 to 9 years.

Harvesting: The seeds are collected when the fruit splits. The scarlet aril is separated and dried in the sun to become mace. The seed is dried in the sun for 2 months, being turned every few days until the kernel rattles within the shell, which is then cracked and removed.

OLOLUIQUE
Rivea corymbosa Hall.;
Morning Glory family (Convolvulaceae)

A slender perennial vine, woody at the base, with 4-inch-long heart-shaped leaves. The flowers are white, in large clusters, 1½ inches wide. The fruit is a one-seeded capsule. Native to tropical America.

Cultivation and Propagation: Cultivate much like the morning glory (which see) except that it is less hardy and should be started indoors in the North. It will also take more water than the common morning glory and, as it is somewhat woody, it can be cut back and brought indoors to carry it over the winter in the North.

Harvesting: The seeds should be gathered as the pods turn brown and dry.

PASSIONFLOWER
Passiflora incarnata L.;
Passionflower family (Passifloraceae)

A strong perennial vine becoming 20 to 30 feet long. The leaves are 3-lobed and deeply toothed. Its flowers are about 2 inches across, white with a purple or pink band around the center. The fruit is yellow when ripe, 1½ to 2 inches long, edible. Native from Virginia south and west to Florida and Texas.

Cultivation and Propagation: This is the hardiest passionflower. If the roots are protected it will survive as far north as the Pennsylvania border. It prefers a light, rich soil, and does well in dry areas. *Passiflora* grows readily from the seed, but takes several weeks to sprout. It is best sown on the surface of light soil or peat moss with bottom heat. The young plants may be planted in the open after 6 months. It may be propagated easily by cuttings of half-ripened growth. These should be about 6 inches long; they will root easily in sand and do not require bottom heat. The vines may eventually overgrow and tangle themselves. Thin them out by cutting branches back to their beginnings. Passionflower dies back at the first frost.

Harvesting: The leaves, stems and flowers may be harvested at any time. This is a good way to keep the plant from crowding itself. Each year before the frost kills it, the entire vine may be cut back to the ground, yielding great quantities of herb. It may be dried in the sun or at a low heat.

PIPILTZINTZINTLI
Salvia divinorum Epling & Jativa;
Mint family (Labiatae)

A woody perennial herb 4 to 6 feet tall with square, hollow stems. The leaves are dark green, 6 to 8 inches long, with toothed edges. The flowers are blue or white on spikes. Only found cultivated by sorcerers in an isolated area in southern Mexico.

Cultivation and Propagation: It is propagated in much the same manner as coleus. It needs a loose, rich soil. It is best grown as a tub plant and brought indoors when the weather begins to cool. It may be grown outdoors in frost-free areas. This salvia is generally grown from cuttings, but I know of one instance in which it was grown from seed. The seed should be germinated in the same way as coleus. Cuttings should be taken in spring, after the plant has had a lot of sun. Cut ½-inch below a node and root in no more than an inch of water. A pinch of rootone may be added to the water and shaken well to dissolve it. This will help prevent stem rot and will stimulate rooting. When the roots are ¼-inch long the cutting should be potted. Longer roots may be damaged. Plant in a 2-inch pot with good potting soil. Grows rapidly after the roots are established. I have found that this plant is susceptible to stem rot if over-watered. It is often attacked by aphids, white flies, spider mites and mealy-bugs.

Harvesting: Harvesting the leaves for use as a hallucinogen should not be attempted until one has at least four one-year-old plants. An equal number of leaves should be harvested from each plant so that the shock to one plant will not be great. Dosage may vary; begin with 10–20 fresh leaves. Fresh leaves are used, as the active principle is believed to be unstable. Considering the rarity of the plant, the leaves should be chewed, because when the juices are expressed much of the active principle is wasted.

PSILOCYBE MUSHROOMS
Agaric family (Agaricaceae)

Many species of mushrooms that contain psilocybin grow wild throughout the American continents, Europe, and parts of Asia and Africa. This book doesn't have the space to provide information on the collection and cultivation of these mushrooms. Cultivation is difficult and collection can be risky if one is not experienced in mycology. The reader who wishes to collect these mushrooms is referred to *Psilocybin: Magic Mushroom Grower's Guide,* from And/Or Press. Information on high-yield cultivation of these mushrooms may be found in *Home Grown Highs* by Mary Jane Superweed. See page 72 for suppliers of these books.

RHYNCHOSIA

Rhynchosia phaseoloides DC;
Bean family (Leguminosae)

A high-climbing, perennial, twining vine with oval, pointed leaves in groups of three. The flowers are reddish-yellow and grow in racemes. The pod contains 2 scarlet seeds with a black end. Native to Central America.

Cultivation and Propagation: *Rhynchosia* may be grown outdoors in California and the South. It is propagated from the seed, which should be nicked and sown in damp peat moss with bottom heat. I have found that the seeds should not be soaked before sowing as this tends to rot them. After sprouting transplant into a rich, well-drained soil in a 2-inch pot. When the temperature outdoors is in the 70s, it may be planted out. In the North, it should be cut back and brought indoors for the winter.

Harvesting: The seeds should be harvested when the pods begin to open.

Note: Rhynchosia seed closely resembles the seed of *Abrus precatorius*, the rosary-pea. *Abrus* seed is one of the most poisonous naturally-occurring substances known to man. Less than one *Abrus* seed, weighing a tenth of a gram, is fatal. However, *Abrus* seed is easily told from *Rhynchosia* seed by the position of the hilum (the small dent where the seed was attached to the pod). In *Abrus* the hilum lies within the *black* part of the seed; in *Rhynchosia* it lies within the *red* part of the seed.

Abrus vines have pinnate leaves with many small leaflets, while *Rhynchosia* leaves are larger and in threes. *Abrus* flowers are red to purple, rarely white; *Rhynchosia* flowers are reddish-yellow.

SAN PEDRO

Trichocereus pachanoi Brit. & Rose;
Cactus family (Cactaceae)

A tall, columnar cactus growing to 18 feet, with 6 to 8 ribs. The spines are small, sometimes nonexistent. The flowers are white, reddish-brown outside, up to 10 inches long, very fragrant, night-blooming. Native to Ecuador and Peru.

Cultivation and Propagation: San Pedro may be grown outdoors in the West and South or as a pot plant in the North. It prefers a sandy, well-drained soil. If potted it should be kept in a clay pot, as this will help the soil dry quickly and prevent root-rot. San Pedro is most easily propagated by cuttings. These should be dried for a few days to several weeks, until the cut surface forms a corky layer. The cutting should then be placed in damp sand, deep enough to support it. After several weeks, when the cactus begins to show signs of growth or swelling, it may be potted in ordinary cactus soil. Seeds are now becoming rare in this country. San Pedro enjoys full sunlight. Seedlings are more light-sensitive than mature plants. If they turn a reddish-brown color, place them in partial shade. Potted cacti should be turned occasionally, to expose all sides to the sun. They are also very sensitive to natural gas and should never be grown in a kitchen with a gas stove. One of the main sources of trouble with potted cacti is over-watering during the dormant months. In winter, the plants' rest period, they should only be watered enough to keep them from shriveling. In summer they may be watered often. San Pedro, like most cacti, tend to grow mostly during spring and summer. During the summer they send their roots deeper into the soil. At this time rootlets may appear at the base of upper branches. This is an ideal time to take cuttings.

Harvesting: A piece of the cactus 3 inches in diameter and 3 to 6 inches long is one dose. To reduce the bulk of the cactus to be eaten, or to store it, it may be sliced thinly and dried quickly in the sun or in an oven at 150° to 225°F. In dry weight the dose should be from 12 to 20 grams. When harvesting, always leave a stump with some areoles (spine pads) on it in the soil, as new columns will grow out of the areoles.

SASSAFRAS

Sassafras albidum; Laurel family (Lauraceae)

Formerly *Sassafras officinale*. Usually a small, slender tree, but sometimes growing 60–100 feet tall. The leaves are ovate, 5 inches long, and sometimes 3-lobed. Its flowers are yellow, in 2-inch-long racemes, followed by a dark blue fruit, on bright red stalks. Native from Maine to Florida and Texas.

Cultivation and Propagation: Sassafras may be easily grown throughout the U.S. in almost any soil. It may be propagated by seeds sown as soon as they are ripe, suckers, and root cuttings. Because of its long tap-roots, it is not easily transplanted when old. In the North it prefers a warm sunny location.

Harvesting: The soil may be cleared away from a portion of the roots and the root-bark peeled away. The inner bark should not be damaged, so that the roots can grow new bark. Another method is to harvest the entire root, as the pith of the root, although weaker, has the same properties as the bark. With any method the tree should be given time to recover and grow new roots before harvesting again.

SHANSI
Coriaria thymifolia Humb. & Bonpl.;
Coriaria family (Coriariaceae)

A shrubby, perennial herb growing from 1 to 4 feet high, with frondlike branches covered with many 1-inch-long leaves. The flowers are very small and grow in drooping, foot-long racemes. Native to Peru and New Zealand.

Cultivation and Propagation: In the South and West this plant may be grown in the open. In colder areas it should be planted at the foot of a south or west wall. In these areas the plant may be killed back to the ground by severe frosts, but may arise from the roots in spring. Shansi will grow well in most well-drained soils if given a sunny location. It is propagated most frequently from seeds sown in early spring, and by green-wood cuttings taken in mid-summer. It may also be propagated by suckers and layers.

Harvesting: When the berries ripen and turn a dark purple they may be harvested and eaten fresh or dried in the sun for use later.

SILVERVINE

Actinidia polygama (Sieb. & Zucc.) Maxim;
Dillenia family (Dilleniaceae)

A perennial, deciduous, twining shrub. The leaves are ovate, up to 6 inches long, often variegated with white or pale yellow. The flowers are white, 5-petaled, ¾-inch across, and occur in June. They are followed by bitter, yellow, many-seeded berries. Native to Japan and China.

Cultivation and Propagation: This plant prefers a rich moist soil, and grows well in a sunny or half-shaded location. It is propagated by seeds which are sown in early spring in pots of sandy soil indoors. It may also be propagated by cuttings of the semi-woody shoots from the current year's growth and rooted in light moist soil in a sheltered place. These cuttings are best taken in July. It can also be propagated by layering the ends of the trailing branches. Give ample water and sturdy supports when well-established. Vines can be guided and tied.

Harvesting: The twigs and young leaves are the part generally used, but older leaves and flowers may also be used. They should be dried as quickly as possible, preferably out of direct sunlight, and without the application of heat.

SINICUICHI
Loosestrife family (Lythraceae)

Two species of *Heimia* are used as hallucinogens. They are:

Heimia myrtifolia Link. Similar to *H. salicifolia,* but much smaller, growing only 3 feet tall. The narrow leaves are 2 inches long, and the yellow flowers are ⅕ of an inch long. Native of Brazil.

H. salicifolia Link. A perennial herbaceous shrub growing to 10 feet tall, with narrow 3½-inch-long leaves. The flowers are yellow, ¾ inch long, and are followed by a ribbed capsule. Native from Mexico to Argentina.

Cultivation and Propagation: These Heimias can be grown outdoors in California and the South. Elsewhere they may be grown as tub plants. Both prefer a well-drained soil, but a good supply of water.

Heimia seed are very small, and should be sown *very* thinly on the surface of fine soil that has previously been firmed with a brick. When dealing with a small quantity of seed, it is best to plant them singly, spacing them an inch apart or more. Do not cover the seed, just press them into the soil with a small flat object. The flat should be watered only by a fine spray or by perfusion from the bottom. Keep the flat somewhat shaded and the surface moist until most of the seeds have germinated. When the first true leaves show, begin exposing the flat to more sun and let the surface dry between waterings. If you have sown them too thickly, either thin out to an inch or so apart or prick them out and space an inch apart in another flat.

Be careful while transplanting, as Heimia seedlings have very large root systems in relation to their size. Seedlings less than ¼-inch tall often have 2-inch-long roots. When the seedlings are an inch or so tall, pot singly, or plant them out to their permanent positions.

Water thoroughly but infrequently to encourage deep rooting. Heimia may also be propagated by cuttings and layers.

Harvesting: The fresh leaves may be harvested after the plant is established well enough to replace the leaves.

SO'KSI
Mirabilis multiflora (Torr.) Gray;
Four O'Clock family (Nyctaginaceae)

An herbaceous perennial, 2 to 3 feet tall, with gray-green, somewhat heart-shaped leaves. The flowers are rose-purple, to 2 inches long, 3 to 6 in each calyx-like involucre. Native to the Southwest; found between 2500 and 5600 feet elevation in Arizona, Utah, Colorado, northern Mexico, and parts of California.

Cultivation and Propagation: This species may be grown as a perennial in the South and West. In the North the roots must be lifted and stored over winter. It prefers a loose, dry, sandy soil but will do well in almost any garden soil provided it is not too damp. The soil should be deep, as this favors the production of large, long roots. So'ksi is propagated by seeds. These are usually sown where the plants are to stand, but they may be sown individually in small pots and set out as soon as the first pair of leaves forms. The seeds often take several weeks to sprout, but the seedlings grow very quickly and form blooming plants in midsummer. The plants should be spaced 15 to 20 inches apart.

Harvesting: The roots may be dug at any time of the year but are preferably dug in the fall, just after frost kills the upper part of the plant. If the roots are left in the ground in the North, they may be destroyed by the cold. Although the roots are large, thick and branching, they break easily and cannot be pulled like carrots. They should be dug with a small trowel or stick, or preferably with the hands. They should be washed thoroughly and dried in the sun before storing. First-year roots weigh up to a pound each.

Note: The roots of a similar plant, the common four o'clock *(Mirabilis jalapa)* are a powerful purgative, and should not be ingested.

SYRIAN RUE
Peganum harmala L.;
Caltrop family (Zygophyllaceae)

A bright green, succulent, perennial herb, becoming woody with age, growing 1 to 2 feet tall. The leaves are 2 inches long and finely divided. The flowers are white, 5-petaled, followed by a 2- to 4-cavitied capsule about ⅜ inch in diameter. Native to the deserts of southern Asia and Africa. Also found wild in some parts of Texas.

Cultivation and Propagation: Syrian rue may be grown outdoors in the South and West. It does well in dry sandy soils, but will benefit from somewhat richer soils. Will stand considerable drought. Viable seed are rare but are the best means of propagation. These should be sown in flats of half sand, half soil, in April and May. Water sparingly, letting the surface dry. The seedlings are very susceptible to overwatering. They should be grown as pot plants the first year, and brought indoors in the winter. In the following spring they may be planted outdoors. In cold-winter areas the roots should be lifted and stored in damp sawdust in a cool place until early spring. Be sure to plant out before new growth starts.

Harvesting: The seed should be gathered as the capsules ripen and should be dried in the sun. The roots may be harvested in autumn, in the same manner as kava roots, after the tops die from frost. These should be split and dried in the sun. The stems and foliage are inactive.

TOBACCO
Nicotiana tabacum L.;
Nightshade family (Solanaceae)

An herbaceous annual growing to 6 feet tall, covered with short, sticky hairs. The leaves are thin, 1 foot or more long. The flowers are rose, purplish-red, or white, 2 inches long, on stalks. Native to tropical America. Possibly a hybrid.

Cultivation and Propagation: Tobacco grows best in a rich, sandy loam. It is easily grown from seed. These should be started in flats of finely sifted soil indoors in the early spring. Because they are very small they should be mixed with sand and sown thinly on the surface of the soil, and lightly pressed in with a small, flat object. The flat should be watered only with a fine spray or perfusion from the bottom. When the seed has germinated move the flat to a sunny position. When the seedlings are large enough to handle they may be transplanted to small pots or moved directly to the garden if the weather is warm enough. The plants should be set out a foot apart in rows 3 feet apart. They should have a warm sunny location with plenty of water when the weather is hot and dry.

Flower buds should be picked off as they appear. This will increase the size and thickness of the leaves. A plant or two may be allowed to flower, because they are beautiful.

Tobacco is susceptible to many insect pests, fungi, and viral blights.

Tobacco is one of the worst soil depleters. After each season the soil in which it has been grown must be heavily fertilized.

Harvesting: The curing of tobacco is an expert business, and will not be covered here. Furthermore, this process greatly reduces its alkaloid content. For hallucinogenic purposes, the leaves should be dried quickly, preferably in the shade or indoors, and without the application of heat. Uncured tobacco is very potent—the Indians who used it would often pass out after as little as one cigarette, and "communicate with the gods." This type of tobacco should be smoked with caution. The danger here is death from overdose rather than addiction. When used as a ritual narcotic it is not smoked often enough to result in addiction.

WILD LETTUCE
Lactuca virosa L.; Sunflower family (Compositae)

A biennial herb growing to 6 feet high. The stem is a smooth, pale green, sometimes spotted with purple. The lower leaves, rising from the base, are from 6 to 18 inches long; the stem leaves are much smaller. The stem is topped by numerous pale yellow flower heads. The seed is black with a tuft of silvery hair. Native to central and southern Europe. Naturalized in the U.S.

Cultivation and Propagation: Wild lettuce prefers a rich, loose, well-drained soil, but can grow almost anywhere if watered frequently. It is propagated by seeds in the same manner as garden lettuce. They may be sown very thickly in rows and thinned out to 18 inches apart, or started in flats in early spring. Flat-grown seedlings should be transplanted very carefully.

Harvesting: The milky juice of this plant may be harvested by cutting off the flower heads and collecting the juice that exudes. This may be repeated several times a day for several weeks by cutting a little off the top each time. Another method that is much easier but will yield less is extracting juice from the entire plant in a vegetable juicer and drying it in the sun or under low heat.

WORMWOOD
Artemisia absinthium L.;
Sunflower family (Compositae)

A hardy perennial, almost shrubby, growing up to 4 feet tall, its spreading branches covered with white, silky hairs. The leaves are much-divided and have an intense, persistent bitter flavor. The flower heads are greenish or yellow, ⅛ inch wide, and very numerous. Its seeds are grayish and very small. Native to Europe and sometimes as an escape in North America.

Cultivation and Propagation: Wormwood grows well in poor, dry sandy soils in a sunny location. The seeds, due to their small size, should be sown in flats where they will not be washed out or packed down by rain. When large enough to be set out they should be planted not closer than 15 inches apart for the first year. The next spring alternate plants should be removed, leaving not less than 30 inches between those remaining. Ripened cuttings may be taken in March or October. These should be set in sandy soil in a shady place and kept moist until well-rooted. It may also be propagated by division of the roots. Weeds should be kept down and the plants should be fertilized very lightly once a year.

Harvesting: The tops and leaves should be gathered and dried in July and August, when the plant is in flower.

Glossary
and
Pronunciation

GLOSSARY

Annual. A plant that naturally completes its life cycle in one year.

Aril. An outer covering of a seed.

Biennial. A plant that lives two years from sowing, usually flowering in the second year.

Capsule. A seed pod that opens when dry and ripe.

Calyx. The small whorl of modified leaves at the base of a flower.

Compound leaves. Leaves divided into two or more leaflets.

Cotyledon. The first leaf or leaves in the seed. In some plants the cotyledons remain underground in the seedcoat.

Germination. The sprouting of a seed.

Heel. A small portion of the previous year's growth at the base of a cutting.

Herbaceous. Dying to the ground or lacking a definite woody structure.

Hilum. The small scar on a seed where it was attached to the seed pod.

Involucre. A whorl of small leaves close underneath a flower or flower cluster.

Layers. See "Propagation".

Leaflet. One part of a compound leaf.

Node. The place on a stem where leaves or branches originate.

Ovate. Having an outline the shape of an egg, with the stalk at the large end.

Perennial. Growing for more than two years. Trees and shrubs are perennials.

Pinching. Removing the terminal bud.

Pinnate. Feather-formed. Said of a compound leaf with the leaflets along both sides of the leaf stalk.

Raceme. An elongated cluster of flowers.

Rhizome. An underground stem.

Sepals. The separate leaves of the calyx.

Suckers. Small plants arising from the base of a larger plant.

Taproot. A primary root growing straight down from a plant.

Terminal. Growing at the end of a branch.

Umbel. A flower cluster in the shape of an umbrella.

Under glass. Grown in the greenhouse or, in the case of a cutting, with a jar placed over it.

PRONUNCIATION

Botanical nomenclature is a language in itself, thrown into a Latin form. Many names are not pronounced according to the rules of classical Latin. The pronunciation guide given below is based on the *Standard Cyclopedia of Horticulture,* and is consistent with standard horticultural pronunciation in most instances.

Accent marks indicate the syllable bearing principal stress and the quality of the accented vowel. A grave accent (`) designates a "long" vowel, and an acute accent (´) designates a short vowel.

The following are the vowel sounds: *à* as in *cane, á* as in *can; è* as in *meet, é* as in *met; ì* as in *pine, í* as in *pin; ò* as in *cone, ó* as in *con; ù* as in *jute, ú* as in *jut; y* is often used as a vowel instead of *i*.

The combination *oi* as in "-oides" is pronounced "oh-EYE-deez"; as an ending it is pronounced "oy." *Ph* is pronounced as *f*. *Ti* followed by a vowel has the sound of "she" as in *Nicotiana* ("ni-koe-she-AY-na") and *Spartium* ("SPAR-she-um"). *Oe* is pronounced as the long *e* in "meet." *Ei* as an ending is pronounced as two syllables, "ay-eye," as in *blumei* ("BLUE-may-eye"). *Ia* as an ending is pronounced "ee-ah," as in *Heimia* ("HI-mee-ah).

The following botanical names appear in the text:

Ábrus precatòrius
Ácorus cálamus
Actinídia polýgama
Arèca cátechu
Argemòne mexicàna
Argyrèia nervòsa
Artemísia absínthium
Átropa belladónna
Calliándra anómala
Càtha edùlis
Catháranthus ròsea
Còleus blùmei
C. pùmilus
Coriària thymifòlia
Coryphántha macromèris
Cýtisus canariénsis
C. scopàrius
Datùra arbòrea
D. candída
D. chlorántha
D. fastuòsa
D. inóxia
D. métel
D. meteloìdes
D. sanguínea
D. stramònium
D. s. var. *tátula*
D. suavèolens
Éphedra nevadénsis
Erythrìna flabellifórmis
Eschschólzia califórnica
Foenículum vulgàre
Genísta canariénsis

GROWING THE HALLUCINOGENS

Heìmia myrtifòlia
H. salicifòlia
Hùmulus lùpulus
Hydrángea paniculàta grandiflòra
Hyoscỳamus nìger
Ìlex paraguayénsis
Iochròma coccíneum
I. fuchsioìdes
I. lanceolàtum
I. tubulòsum
Ipomoèa trícolor
I. violàcea
Kaempfèria galánga
Lactùca vìrosa
Leonòtis leonùrus
Lobèlia inflàta
Mandrágora officinàrum
Merrémia tuberòsa
Mirábilis multiflòra
Myrística fràgrans
Népeta catària
Nicotiàna tabácum
Passiflòra incarnàta
Pegánum hármala
Pìper methýsticum
Podophýllum peltàtum
Rhynchòsia phaseoloìdes
Rivèa corymbòsa
Sálvia divinórum
Sássafras álbidum
S. officinàle
Sóphora secundiflòra
Spártium júnceum

Trichocèreus páchanoi
Turnèra diffùsa
Vínca ròsea

Glossary and Pronunciation

Printed in the USA
CPSIA information can be obtained
at www.ICGtesting.com
JSHW082224140824
68134JS00015B/727

9 780914 171478